TUNING GUIDES.

No. 17. For Violin.

No.
17. German Silver, key of E, A, D, and G, for tuning violin or mandolin 50c
18. German Silver, key of B, G sharp, E, A and E, for tuning banjo 60c
26. German silver, key of E, B, G, D, A and E, for tuning guitar.. 70c

TUNING PIPES.

No.   No. 8.   Each.
8. German silver, key of A .... $ .15
9. German silver, key of C .... .15
10. German silver, key of A and C combined .... .25
20. German silver, with sliding reed, producing chromatic scale 1.25

MUSIC STANDS.
Folding Iron, Japanned and Nickel Plated

No.
1. Ideal, concave, mal'ble steel feet, black japanned, weight 35 oz..90c.
2. Ideal, better quality, smoother finish, heavily nickel plated......$1.75
3. Perfection, top adjustable to any angle, black japanned........60c.
4. Perfection, better quality, smoother finish, highly nickel plated..1.75
5. Telescope, full nickel plated,lgth when shut up, 14 in., weight 15 oz., in black leather case.........$4.50

Nos. 3 and 4.

CLARIONETS.

Instruction book free. Always mention what key wanted. Made in key of A, B, C, D or E.
No. 1. Boxwood, natural color, 6 brass keys, horn trimmed......................$3.45
No. 6. Boxwood, natural color, 10 brass keys, horn trimmed.......................5.75
No. 11. Grenadillo, 13 German silver keys, German silver trimmed..................12.35
No. 16. Grenadillo, Albert system, 13 Ger. silver keys, 2 rings, cork joints, Ger. silver trimmed 15.75
No. 26. Grenadillo, Albert system, 13 German silver keys, with trill keys (C and B), 2 rings, German silver trimmed..23.75

STRINGS.

No. 1. Violin strings, best Italian, polished, per set of 4 .... 80c
No. 2. Steel violin strings, 1 length, silver plated, best quality, full set of 4 strings...... 20c
No. 7. Gut Banjo strings, full set of 5, best quality, per set 40c
No. 181. Steel banjo strings, full set of 5 .... 25c
No. 13. Gut guitar strings, full set of 6 .... 50c
No. 21. Steel guitar strings, full set of 6 .... 35c
No. 5. Mandolin strings, silvered wire, full set of 8 .... 45c

MUSIC STAND CASES.

1. Sole leather, for folding iron stands................... $1.00

"UNIVERSAL" PATENT ADJUSTABLE TUNING FORK.

The feature of changing the pitch makes our fork the only reliable gauge of sound in the world, that is adapted to any locality or country, as indicated by the name "Universal."

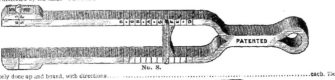

No. 8.
No. 8. Nicely done up and boxed, with directions..each, 75c

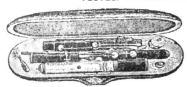

Nos. 2 and 3.
No. 2. Steel, key of A, philharmonic .... each, 15c   No. 3. Steel, key of C, philharmonic .... each, 15c
No. 6. Blued Steel, key of A, superior quality....... " 25c   No. 7. Blued Steel, key of C, superior quality.... " 25c

BATONS.

No. 1. White holly, tapering, plain .... each, 50c

No. 2. Rosewood, German silver ferrules ....each, $1.00
No. 3. White holly and ebony handle, tapering, very rich, German silver ferrules................... 1.50

FLUTES.—INSTRUCTION BOOK FREE WITH EACH FLUTE.

No.   Each.
104. D, 1 key with slide, German silver trimmed, in paper case...............$1.75
49. D, 4 keys, cocoa, German silver rings and slide, in paper case............. 2.75
44. D, 6 keys, Grenadillo, German silver rings and slide, in paper case......... 3.90
116. D, 8 keys, Grenadillo, German silver rings and slide, in leather case......... 8.00
164. D, 13 keys, Grenadillo, ivory head, with slide, in fine case, like illustration 17.50

No. 164.

Music to Christian people is like a mother to her child. Take music from the Church, and you make her an orphan.

C. E. LESLIE,
195 Wabash Ave.,
Chicago, Ill.

Correspondence solicited.

Copyright, 1891, by C. E. Leslie.

4 NOT A SPARROW FALLETH. Continued.

NEAR THE CROSS. Continued.

NEAR THE CROSS. Concluded.

BEHOLD! I STAND AT THE DOOR.

C. E. LESLIE.

BEHOLD! I STAND AT THE DOOR. Continued.

11

12 BEHOLD! I STAND AT THE DOOR. Continued.

BEHOLD! I STAND AT THE DOOR. Concluded. 13

THE BEAUTIFUL CITY OF GOD.

C. E. LESLIE

THE BEAUTIFUL CITY OF GOD. Continued. 15

16 THE BEAUTIFUL CITY OF GOD. Continued.

THE BEAUTIFUL CITY OF GOD. Concluded.

20 TAKE ME TO THY CARE. Continued.

TAKE ME TO THY CARE. Concluded.

HYMN ANTHEM.

C. E. LESLIE.

Grace, 'tis a charm-ing sound, Har-mo-nious to the ear, Har-

mo-nious to the ear; Heav-en with its ech-o shall re-

sound, And all the earth shall hear. Grace, 'tis a charming

sound, Har-mo-nious to the ear, Har-mo-nious to the ear;

Heav-en with its ech-o shall re-sound, And all the earth shall hear.

Grace first con-trived the way To save re-bell-ious man,
Grace first con-trived the way To save re-bell-ious man,

HYMN ANTHEM. Concluded. 23

HEAR US, O FATHER.

C. E. LESLIE.

HEAR US, O FATHER. Continued. 25

THE LORD HIS LIFE DID GIVE.

E. R. Latta.   C. E. Leslie.

28   THE LORD HIS LIFE DID GIVE. Continued.

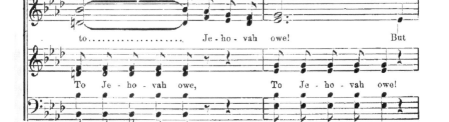

30 — THE CHRIST IS COME.

Good for Christmas or any Service.

LAURA E. NEWELL.

C. E. LESLIE

Hail, all hail, In your hearts pre - pare him room,

Hail, all hail, the Christ is come! In your hearts pre - pare him room;

Let your voice Wel -come Christ, re - ceive your King;

Let your voice in an-thems ring, Wel -come Christ, re - ceive your King;

Yes, near and far,

Sound the ti- dings near and far, For Christ is come, our guid - ing

Yes, near and far.

THE CHRIST IS COME. Concluded. 33

36 BEYOND. Continued.

BEYOND. Concluded. 37

38 YE SHALL FIND REST.

OUR RISEN LORD.

Good for Easter or other Services.

ARR. BY C. E. LESLIE FROM
BILLINGS

Hal - le - lu - jah! The

The Lord is ris - en in - deed! Hal - le - lu - jah!

Lord is ris - en in - deed! Hal - le - lu - jah!

Hal - le - lu - jah! Now is

Christ ris - en from the dead, and be-come the first fruits of them that slept;

Now is Christ, The first fruits of

Now is Christ ris - en from the dead, and be-come The first fruits of

OUR RISEN LORD. Continued. 47

48 OUR RISEN LORD. Continued.

HE WILL HAVE MERCY. Continued 51

52   HE WILL HAVE MERCY. Continued.

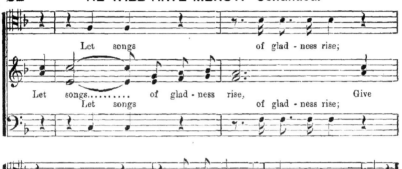

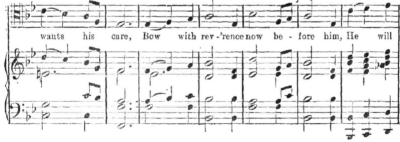

HE WILL HAVE MERCY. Concluded. 53

THE GARDEN OF THE LORD.

C. E. LESLIE.

THE GARDEN OF THE LORD. Continued. 55

ENTER YE IN AT THE STRAIT GATE.

58 ENTER YE IN AT THE STRAIT GATE. Continued.

ENTER YE IN AT THE STRAIT GATE. Concluded.

Send for

The Memorial Offering,

A Splendid collection of Music for Funeral occasions.

The Chicago Music Co.,

195 & 197 WABASH AVE.,   CHICAGO, ILL.

60   PRAISE THE LORD.

E. M. HERNDON.

PRAISE THE LORD. Continued.

62 PRAISE THE LORD. Continued.

PRAISE THE LORD. Concluded. 63

HEAR OUR PRAYER. Continued. 65

HEAR OUR PRAYER. Continued.

HEAR OUR PRAYER. Concluded.

THE LORD WILL COMFORT ZION.   71

ALFRED BEIRLY.

72 THE LORD WILL COMFORT ZION. Continued.

THE LORD WILL COMFORT ZION. Concluded. 73

74 THE MERCY SEAT. H. W. FAIRBANK.

THE MERCY SEAT. Continued. 75

76 THE MERCY SEAT. Continued.

THE MERCY SEAT. Concluded. 77

80 PRAISE THE LORD.

C. E. LESLIE.

82 PRAISE THE LORD. Concluded.

FATHER, WE COME.

A. R. Churchill.

COME SOUND HIS PRAISE. Continued.   87

at   his throne, Come bow   be - fore   the Lord;   We   are his work and

at   his throne, Come bow   be - fore   the Lord;   We   are his work and

not   our own;   He formed us   by   his word.   To - day,   to - day at -

not   our own;   He formed us   by   his word.   To - day,   to - day at -

tend   his voice, Nor dare,   nor dare pro - voke   his rod, Come, like the peo - ple

tend   his voice, Nor dare,   nor dare pro - voke   his rod, Come, like the peo - ple

of   his choice, And own your gra - cious God,   And   own your gra - cious God.

of   his choice, And own your gra - cious God,   And   own your gra - cious God.

I WILL EXTOL THEE. Concluded.

94 THE LORD IS MY FOUNDATION. Continued.

THE LORD IS MY FOUNDATION. Concluded. 95

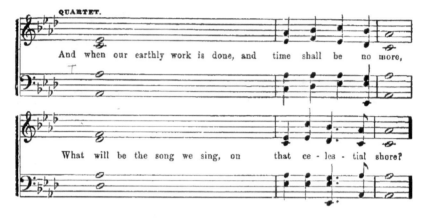

98 ON THE MOUNTAIN'S TOP. Continued.

DAUGHTER OF ZION.

ALFRED BEIRLY.

DAUGHTER OF ZION. Concluded.

THE LORD HATH SPOKEN.

C. E. LESLIE.

The Lord hath spo-ken peace to my soul, The Lord hath spo-ken

peace to my soul, He hath blessed me a-bund-ant-ly, Hath par-doned my

sins; He hath shown me great mer-cy and saved me by his love.

DUET. Soprano & Tenor.

I will sing of his good-ness and mer-cy while I live, And for-

And for-

116 SWEET IS THE WORK. Continued.

122 HARK! THOSE HOLY VOICES. Concluded.

126 THE KING OF LOVE.

A. BEIRLY.

THE KING OF LOVE. Concluded. 129

I HAVE SET WATCHMEN.

FRANK M. DAVIS.

I have set watch-men up-on thy walls, I have set watch-men up-on thy walls, I have set watch-men up-on thy walls, O, Je-ru-sa-lem!

Nev-er hold their peace, Which shall never hold their peace, Which shall never hold their ru-sa-lem! Nev-er hold their peace,

Nev-er hold their peace, Never hold their peace, Day nor night, day nor night.

peace, Nev-er hold their peace, Day nor night, day nor night
Nev-er hold their peace,

I HAVE SET WATCHMEN. Continued. 131

132   I HAVE SET WATCHMEN. Concluded.

OUR FALLEN COMRADES.

For Decoration or Funeral Services of a Soldier.

E. R. LATTA.   C. E. LESLIE.

1. Oh, ye who left your peaceful homes, The battle field to try,
2. How clasped the hands of loved ones then! And scarce an eye was dry!
3. How did the wives and mothers grieve, And little chil-dren cry,
4. Ye fought and fell, the land to save, Beneath a storm-y sky;
5. May heaven bless the sacred soil Where our brave com-rades lie;

How were your hearts with anguish rent, The day ye said good-by, good-by!
And not a smile lit up the face, The day ye said good-by, good-by!
What blackness did the spirit shroud, The day ye said good-by, good-by!
No friend was near to ease the pain, No one to say good-by, good-by!
May we all meet in heaven above, No more to say good-by, good-by!

JOY AND PEACE. Continued. 135

136 JOY AND PEACE. Continued.

JOY AND PEACE. Concluded. 137

138 THOU WILT KEEP HIM.

C. D. AMSTUTZ.

THOU WILT KEEP HIM. Continued. 139

140   THOU WILT KEEP HIM. Concluded.

REMEMBER ME.   FRANK M. DAVIS.

REMEMBER ME. Concluded. 141

144   O SING UNTO THE LORD A NEW SONG.

P. W. HILL.

By permission.

O SING UNTO THE LORD. Continued. 145

146 O SING UNTO THE LORD. Concluded.

BE YE PREPARED. Concluded. 149

150   LORD, HAVE MERCY.

Arr. from MOZART, by F. R. BETTIS.

LORD, HAVE MERCY. Continued.

151

LORD, HAVE MERCY. Concluded. 153

154 GUIDE MY STEPS TO THE PORTALS.

Arr. from "Christian the Pilgrim."

Copyright, 1883, by The Chicago Music Co.

156 GUIDE MY STEPS. Continued.

158. THE LORD HATH ASCENDED ON HIGH.

P. W. HILL.

THE LORD HATH ASCENDED. Concluded. 159

Contents.

A
Abide with me.................................... 41

B
Behold, I stand at the door.................... 10
Be ye prepared................................... 147
Beyond... 35
Blessed is he..................................... 44

C
Come sound his praise........................... 86

D
Daughter of Zion.................................. 100

E
Enter ye in at the strait gate................... 57

F
Father, we come.................................. 83

G
Guide my steps to the portals................... 154

H
Hark, those holy voices.......................... 120
Hear our prayer................................... 64
Hear us, O Father................................. 24
Heavenward.. 34
He will have mercy................................ 50
Hymn Anthem..................................... 23

I
I have set watchman.............................. 130
I love to tell the story........................... 143
In heavenly love.................................. 142
I will extol thee.................................. 89

J
Jesus, lover of my soul........................... 118
Joy and peace..................................... 133

L
Lord have mercy.................................. 150

M
Magnify the Lord.................................. 107

N
Near the cross..................................... 6
Not a sparrow falleth............................. 3

O
O come let us worship............................ 123
O sing unto the Lord a new song................ 144
Our fallen comrades.............................. 132
Our risen Lord.................................... 46
On the mountain's top appearing................ 96

P
Praise the Lord (No. 1.).......................... 60
Praise the Lord (No. 2.).......................... 80

R
Remember me..................................... 146

S
Sing Jehovah's praises........................... 104
Sweet is the work................................. 115

T
Take me to thy care.............................. 18
The beautiful city of God......................... 14
The Christ is come................................ 30
The garden of the Lord........................... 54
The king of love.................................. 126
The Lord his life did give........................ 27
The Lord hath spoken............................. 112
The Lord hath ascended on high.................. 158
The Lord is my foundation........................ 93
The Lord will comfort Zion....................... 71
The mercy seat.................................... 74
The Shepherd's voice.............................. 78
Thou wilt keep him................................ 138

Y
Ye shall find rest.................................. 39

H. S. BIGELOW, MUSIC TYPOGRAPHER, CHICAGO.

SOLO B♭ CORNET.

No.   With Double Water Key and German Silver Mouthpiece.
3000. Brass ....each, $11.40 3002. Triple nickel plated, each, $19.00

CORNET CASES.

No. 32. Brown canvas, leather bound, flannel lined, with shoulder
strap...each, $1.50
No. 14. Wood, black, varnished, lined, with lock, handle and hooks. " 1.50
No. 31. Leather, russet color, satchel form, red flannel lined, nickel-
plated trimmings with shoulder strap..................... " 1.55

Nos. 37 and 40.

GUITARS.

INSTRUCTION BOOK FREE WITH EACH GUITAR.

No.   WITH PATENT HEADS.
15. Imported Guitar. Maple, red shaded, good quality..$6.15
81. Imported Guitar. Maple, shaded, dark, fine
    quality, inlaid sound hole........................ 4.95
90. Imported Guitar. Imitation rosewood, white
    edges, large size................................. 6.50

American Guitars. Superb finish, scale absolutely correct, and warranted against splitting. Necks are made of Spanish
No.   cedar, and the finger boards of rosewood.
37. A beautiful finished solid mahogany guitar...each,$ 9.00
40. A beautiful finished solid rosewood guitar..   "   11.90
36. A beautiful finished solid maple guitar.....   "   7.00

GUITAR CASES.

60. Brown canvas, leather bound, with opening at
    end..each, $2.75
 2. Green felt, for either standard or concert size
    guitars....................................each, 1.50

MANDOLINS.

This instrument is becoming very popular, which is evidenced by the increased demand for it. We would state for the benefit of those desirous of learning to play the mandolin that they are "tuned" and fingered the same as a violin, so that one who can play a violin may easily learn to perform on the mandolin.

AMERICAN MANDOLINS.—THE "NELSON."

No. 1. These instruments are of our own manufacture, and guaranteed to be absolutely correct scale, and to not split or warp out of shape. Eleven maple ribs, with mahogany band, Spanish cedar neck, rosewood finger board.....each, $7.00

THE LELAND.—Professional Mandolin.

No. 3. Patent head, narrow maple and rosewood ribs, inlaid sound hole, with fancy
guard...each, $12.00

No.   **MANDOLIN CASES.**
70. Brown canvas, leather bound, flannel lined, with strap fastening.........each, $0.25
69. Embossed solid sole leather, hand sewed, good quality.................... "   5.00

No. 3.

Nos. 8, 9 and 10.

All have nickel hoops, wood lined, walnut necks, raised frets, polished pegs.
No.   Each.
 8. 18 nickel-plated hexagon
    brackets, nickel shell, wood
    lined, wired edge, raised
    frets, 11-inch.................. $4.50
 7. 21 nickel-plated hexagon
    brackets........................ 5.40
 9. 25 nickel-plated hexagon
    brackets........................ 6.50
10. 31 nickel-plated hexagon
    brackets........................ 7.00
19. 39 nickel-plated hexagon
    brackets........................ 7.50
11. Same as No. 10, with white
    celluloid pegs.................. 8.00

No.   **ARTISTS' BANJOS.**
18. The Leland, 11-inch nickel
    shell, wood lined, wired
    edge, French polished ma-
    hogany neck, with ebony
    finger board, handsome
    pearl inlaying, with large
    metal name plate at bottom
    of finger board, rabbeted
    strainer hoop, metal stay
    piece, patent "Crown"
    tail piece, 31 nickel-plated
    hexagon brackets............... 10.00

BANJO CASES.—No. 8. Brown canvas, leather bound, flannel lined,
opening at end..................... $6.50
No. 4. Green Felt bags, to fit shapes for
11 or 12 inch banjo................ 1.25

Printed in the USA
CPSIA information can be obtained
at www.ICGtesting.com
LVHW011204111023
760586LV00069B/818